A Scots Yearbook

LOMOND BOOKS

Back cover photograph, *Red deer stag,* courtesy of Neil McIntyre and
front cover photograph, *Invercauld Bridge and the River Dee, Braemar, Aberdeenshire,*
courtesy of Dennis Hardley

Scenes of town, country and historic interest courtesy of Dennis Hardley except
The Auld Kirk, Alloway, courtesy of Ayrshire and Arran Tourist Board and
Edinburgh Castle Fireworks, courtesy of Philip Hawkins

Scottish wildlife photographs courtesy of Neil McIntyre:
Red squirrel
Puffin
Grey seal pup
Red grouse
Golden eagle
Red deer stags
Mountain hare

This edition published 1999 by Geddes & Grosset,
for Lomond Books Ltd.

© 1999 Geddes & Grosset,
David Dale House, New Lanark ML11 9DJ, Scotland.
Reprinted 2001, 2002

ISBN 0 947782 24 9

Printed and bound in Poland, OZGraf S.A.

The Great Glen, as seen from the shore of Loch Oich near Invergarry, Highland

January

1

2

3

4

5

6

7

Notes

January

8

9

10

11

12

13

14

Notes

Killin, at the head of Loch Tay, Stirling District

15

19

16

20

17

21

18

Notes

*The Forth Road
Bridge, linking
South Queensferry,
Edinburgh, with
North Queensferry,
Fife*

22

23

24

25

26

27

28

Notes

Ben Lomond, as seen from across Loch Ard, Stirling District

January/February

29

2

30

3

31

4

1

Notes

5

9

6

10

7

11

8

Notes

Shepherd's cottage amongst the Glen Coe hills, Highland

February

12

16

13

17

14

18

15

Notes

19

23

20

24

21

25

22

Notes

Puffin

February/March

26

27

28/29

1

2

3

4

Notes

Tam o' Shanter
A Tale
(Extract)

Of Brownyis and Bogillis full
is this Buke.
Gawin Douglas

When chapmen billies leave the
   street,
And drouthy neebors, neebors meet,
As market-days are wearing late,
An' folk begin to tak the gate;
While we sit bousing at the nappy,
And getting fou and unco happy,
We think na on the lang Scots
   miles,
The mosses, water, slaps, and
   styles,
That lie between us and our hame,
Whare sits our sulky, sullen dame,
Gathering her brows like gathering
   storm,
Nursing her wrath to keep it warm.

This truth fand honest Tam o'
   Shanter,
As he frae Ayr ae night did canter,
(Auld Ayr, wham ne'er a town
   surpasses
For honest men and bonie lasses.)

Robert Burns

Auld Kirk,
Alloway,
South Ayrshire

5

9

6

10

7

11

8

Notes

*Rothesay Castle,
Isle of Bute, Argyll
and Bute*

12

16

13

17

14

18

15

Notes

March

19

20

21

22

23

24

25

Notes

26

30

27

31

28

1

29

Notes

April

2

6

3

7

4

8

5

Notes

Balvenie Castle, near Dufftown, Moray

9

13

10

14

11

15

12

Notes

16

20

17

21

18

22

19

Notes

23

24

25

26

27

28

29

Notes

30

4

1

5

2

6

3

Notes

May

7

8

9

10

11

12

13

Notes

Edinburgh Castle, viewed from Princes Street Gardens

14

18

15

19

16

20

17

Notes

*Ramsey Garden,
above The Mound,
Edinburgh*

May

21

25

22

26

23

27

24

Notes

May/June

28

1

29

2

30

3

31

Notes

Dunrobin Castle,
near Golspie,
Highland

June

4

8

5

9

6

10

7

Notes

A Red, Red Rose
Tune: Major Graham

O my luve's like a red, red rose
   That's newly sprung in June;
O my luve's like the melodie
   That's sweetly play'd in tune.

As fair art thou, my bonie lass,
   So deep in luve am I;
And I will luve thee still, my dear,
   Till a' the seas gang dry.

Till a' the seas gang dry, my dear,
   And the rocks melt wi' the sun:
O I will luve thee still, my dear,
   While the sands o' life shall run.

And fare-thee-weel, my only luve,
   And fare-thee-weel awhile!
And I will come again, my luve,
   Tho' 'twere ten thousand mile!

Robert Burns

June

11

12

13

14

15

16

17

Notes

June

18

19

20

21

22

23

24

Notes

25

29

26

30

27

1

28

Notes

July

2

3

4

5

6

7

8

Notes

Findochty, on the Moray coast, Moray

9

13

10

14

11

15

12

Notes

*Beach near
Durness,
Sutherland,
Highland*

16

20

17

21

18

22

19

Notes

Inverness Castle, by the River Ness, Highland

July

23

24

25

26

27

28

29

Notes

30

3

31

4

1

5

2

Notes

August

6

7

8

9

10

11

12

Notes

13

17

14

18

15

19

16

Notes

August

20

21

22

23

24

25

26

Notes

*The Forth
Railway Bridge
spanning the
Firth of Forth
and linking
Edinburgh and
Fife*

27

31

28

1

29

2

30

Notes

Verses Written with a Pencil
over the chimney-piece, in the parlour of
the Inn at Kenmore, Taymouth (Extract)

Admiring Nature in her wildest grace,
These northern scenes with weary feet I trace;
O'er many a winding dale and painful steep,
Th' abodes of coveyed grouse and timid sheep,
My savage journey, curious, I pursue,
Till fam'd Breadalbaine opens to my view.
The meeting cliffs each deep-sunk glen divides,
The woods, wild-scattered, clothe their ample
    sides;

Th' outstretching lake, embosomed 'mong the
    hills,
The eye with wonder and amazement fills;
The Tay, meandering sweet in infant pride,
The palace, rising on his verdant side;
The lawns, wood-fringed in Nature's native taste;
The hillocks, dropt in Nature's careless haste;
The arches, striding o'er the new-born stream;
The village, glittering in the noontide beam—

Robert Burns

3

7

4

8

5

9

6

Notes

10

11

12

13

14

15

16

Notes

Castle Stalker,
Loch Laich,
Appin, Argyll
and Bute

17

21

18

22

19

23

20

Notes

24

28

25

29

26

30

27

Notes

Tantallon Castle and the Bass Rock, near North Berwick, East Lothian

October

1

2

3

4

5

6

7

Notes

October

8

9

10

11

12

13

14

Notes

15

19

16

20

17

21

18

Notes

Loch Lochy, near Gairlochy, Highland

October

22

23

24

25

26

27

28

Notes

Loch Awe at sunset, Argyll and Bute

29

2

30

3

31

4

1

Notes

November

5

9

6

10

7

11

8

Notes

Winter view looking southwest from the shore of Loch Laggan, near Inverness, Highland

12

13

14

15

16

17

18

Notes

*Ben Nevis and
Loch Eil from
Corpach,
Highland*

November

19

20

21

22

23

24

25

Notes

*River Luineag,
near Glenmore,
Highland*

November/December

26

30

27

1

28

2

29

Notes

December

3

7

4

8

5

9

6

Notes

December

10

11

12

13

14

15

16

December

17

21

18

22

19

23

20

Notes

Auld Lang Syne

For auld lang syne, my jo,
For auld lang syne,
We'll tak a cup o' kindness yet,
For auld lang syne.

Should auld acquaintance be forgot
And never brought to mind?
Should auld acquaintance be forgot,
And auld lang syne?

And surely ye'll be your pint-stoup!
And surely I'll be mine;
And we'll tak a cup o' kindness yet,
For auld lang syne.

We twa hae run about the braes,
And pou'd the gowans fine;
But we've wander'd mony a weary fit,
Sin' auld lang syne.

We twa hae paidl'd in the burn,
Frae morning sun till dine;
But seas between us braid hae roar'd,
Sin' auld lang syne.

And there's a hand, my trusty fiere!
And gie's a hand o' thine!
And we'll tak a right gude-willie
   waught,
For auld lang syne.

Robert Burns

Edinburgh Castle
Fireworks

December

24

28

25

29

26

30

27

31

Addresses & Telephone Numbers

Addresses & Telephone Numbers

Addresses & Telephone Numbers

Addresses & Telephone Numbers

Addresses & Telephone Numbers MNO

Addresses & Telephone Numbers

Addresses & Telephone Numbers

Addresses & Telephone Numbers

Addresses & Telephone Numbers

Addresses & Telephone Numbers